Kiel

Holidays

Arbor Day

By Kelly Bennett

Consultant
Nanci R. Vargus, Ed.D.
Assistant Professor
Literacy Education
University of Indianapolis
Indianapolis, Indiana

New Yor   Sydney
Me   g
Danbury, Connecticut

Designer: Herman Adler Design
Photo Researcher: Caroline Anderson
The photo on the cover shows a boy planting a tree on Arbor Day.

Library of Congress Cataloging-in-Publication Data

Bennett, Kelly.
  Arbor Day / by Kelly Bennett.
    p. cm. — (Rookie read-about holidays)
Summary: A simple introduction to the traditions and festivities of
Arbor Day.
  ISBN 0-516-22861-7 (lib. bdg.)   0-516-27754-5 (pbk.)
  1. Arbor Day—United States—Juvenile literature. [1. Arbor Day.
2. Holidays.] I. Title. II. Series.
  SD363 .B46 2003
  394.262—dc21
                                        2002015135

Plant a tree for Arbor Day!

4

"Arbor" is another word for tree. Arbor Day could also be called "Tree Day."

It is a day to remember the beauty and importance of trees.

The first Arbor Day was
in 1872. It was the idea
of J. Sterling Morton.

He saw people cutting down many trees. He was afraid the forests would disappear. He wanted people to plant more trees.

April 2003

Sunday	Monday	Tuesday	Wednesday	Thursday	Friday	Saturday
		1	2	3	4	5
6	7	8	9	10	11	12
13	14	15	16	17	18	19
20	21	22	23	24	25	26
27	28	29	30			

National Arbor Day is the last Friday in April.

Some states celebrate during their best tree-planting time.

When is Arbor Day in your state?

Trees make a gas called oxygen. We need oxygen to breathe.

Trees shade us from the sun. Tree roots keep soil from washing away in the rain.

12

Sometimes we burn wood to keep warm.

Long ago, people had to cook over wood fires.

Have you ever cooked over a campfire?

We eat apples, nuts, cherries, and other foods that grow on trees.

Insects eat tree leaves. So do giraffes and other animals.

The sap from sugar maple
trees gives us maple syrup.

Gloves, tires, and rubber
bands are made from
rubber-tree sap.

Trees also give us paper.
Logs are ground into sawdust.
The sawdust is made into
a wet mixture called pulp.

Sawdust

Pulp

The pulp is put through
heavy rollers to make paper.

People build homes
out of wood.

Trees are home for birds and squirrels. Beavers build homes from branches and mud.

How can you celebrate
Arbor Day?

Share stories, poems, jokes,
and songs about trees.

Draw pictures of trees.

Have a tree hunt. Look
for the biggest tree or the
smallest tree.

Find trees with colorful or funny-shaped leaves.

Many people plant trees
on Arbor Day.

A grown-up can help
you get a tree seedling.

Plant your seedling
outside. Care for it
and watch it grow.

Trees give us so
many things.

Thank you, trees!

Words You Know

campfire

forest

insect

logs

maple syrup

pulp

sap

sawdust

seedling

Index

About the Author

Kelly Bennett has written six books for children. She likes to have adventures with her son, Max, and her daughter, Alexis. She lives in Katy, Texas.

Photo Credits

Photographs © 2003: Corbis Images: cover (Gary Braasch), 29 (Mark E. Gibson), 7, 30 bottom right (Lake County Museum), 18, 31 center left (Dan Lamont), 24 (Galen Rowell); Dembinsky Photo Assoc.: 25 top left, 25 bottom right, 25 bottom left (Michael P. Gadomski), 18, 31 bottom left (Mark E. Gibson), 11 (Richard Hamilton Smith); Nebraska State Historical Society: 6; Peter Arnold Inc.: 4, 30 top right (Kerry Brill/UNEP), 21 (Steve Kaufman), 19 (Tom Hollyman), 16, 31 center right (Blair Seitz), 16 inset, 31 top (Michael Newman), 26 (Jonathan Nourok), 14 (David Young-Wolff); Stock Boston: 3, 31 bottom right (Bob Daemmrich), 23 (Frank Siteman); The Image Works: 12, 30 top left (Bob Daemmrich), 17 (Kathy McLaughlin); Visuals Unlimited: 15 left, 30 bottom left (WM Banaszewski), 25 top right (Ray Dove), 20 (Mark Gibson); Wildlife Collection/D. Robert Franz: 15.